PORTRAIT OF
ROBIN HOOD COUNTRY

JANET AND PETER ROWORTH

HALSGROVE

First published in Great Britain in 2009

Copyright words © Janet and Peter Roworth 2009
Photographs © Roworth images 2009

Title page photograph: An oak tree symbol taken from the sign for Thoresby Colliery.

Introduction page photograph: Leaves and acorns litter the ground under the oak trees of Sherwood Forest.

British Library Cataloguing-in-Publication Data
A CIP record for this title is available from the British Library

ISBN 978 1 84114 707 9

HALSGROVE
Halsgrove House,
Ryelands Industrial Estate,
Bagley Road, Wellington, Somerset TA21 9PZ
Tel: 01823 653777   Fax: 01823 216796
email: sales@halsgrove.com

Part of the Halsgrove group of companies
Information on all Halsgrove titles is available at: www.halsgrove.com

Printed and bound by Grafiche Flaminia, Italy

INTRODUCTION

Sherwood Forest is the legendary home of Robin Hood and his band of Merry Men and in the past it covered a large part of Nottinghamshire. However, Sherwood was never continuous thick forest, rather there were areas of oak and birch woodland separated by open heath and rough grassland. In medieval times herds of deer and wild boar roamed the forest and they were protected so that they could be hunted by the king. The infertile, sandy soils were not suited to arable farming but the woodland and heath were grazed by cattle, sheep and pigs.

Over the centuries much of the woodland was cleared, the timber being used for house and ship building. Monastic houses were founded at Rufford, Welbeck and Newstead and their estates took over considerable areas of Sherwood. After Henry VIII dissolved the monasteries their estates passed into the hands of members of the aristocracy. Over the next two centuries these powerful Nottinghamshire landowners converted the monastic buildings into prestigious country houses and surrounded them with landscaped parkland. The Dukeries came to be the name for the part of the county that contained the estates of four dukes. Worksop Manor was the property of the Duke of Norfolk. Welbeck Abbey belonged to the Duke of Portland. The Dukes of Newcastle owned Clumber Park, and Thoresby Hall was the seat of the Dukes of Kingston. Although never quite achieving a dukedom the Savile family of Rufford Abbey could be considered the fifth honorary member of The Dukeries.

Worksop Manor is now in private hands and it is closed to the public. The splendid house and grounds at Welbeck Abbey also remain in private hands but the Robin Hood Way, a long-distance trail that runs from Nottingham Castle to Edwinstowe, passes through the parkland. Part of the former walled garden is used as a garden centre and farm shop, while the former gas works for the estate have been converted into the Harley Gallery which houses the Portland Collection and displays of contemporary visual art and craft.

Clumber Park was developed by the Dukes of Newcastle who built a fine mansion, several lodges at the various gated entrances, and created the lake and gardens. In the nineteenth century thousands of trees were planted in the park, including the Lime Avenue along the entrance from Apleyhead Gate. By the 1930s the great country house era was over and the estate was in decline. The house contents were sold and the house was demolished in 1938. During the Second World War the park was used to store ammunition and as a training ground for troops. In 1946 the National Trust, aided by public subscriptions, purchased the estate. It now provides 1,500 hectares of wonderful wood and parkland for visitors to enjoy, and the facilities include a shop, restaurant, cycle hire and a caravan and camping site.

The present Thoresby Hall was built in 1860, replacing an earlier house. It has recently been fully restored as a hotel. The adjacent stableyard has been converted into the Courtyard Gallery with shops and a café, while the surrounding parkland is open for walkers.

Rufford Abbey began life as a Cistercian monastery but in the sixteenth century it passed to the Talbot family and then to the Saviles. The abbey buildings were converted into a fine country house which, over the centuries, was extended and improved. However the estate was sold in 1938 and during the Second World War it was occupied by the Army. In 1952 the house and park, now in a neglected condition, was purchased by Nottinghamshire County Council, and it was found necessary to demolish the unsafe parts of the building. Then in 1969 the grounds were declared a Country Park and many of the buildings have been restored to provide visitor facilities. Today the stable block houses a gallery and Ceramics Centre, and there are tea rooms and a restaurant. The Orangery, which began life as a bath house, is used to display outdoor sculptures and there are further examples throughout the gardens.

In the nineteenth century the remnants of the ancient oak woods of Sherwood Forest formed part of the Thoresby Estate. Romantic Victorian writers sparked a new interest in the Robin Hood legends, and this drew tourists to the area. In 1954 Birklands and Bilhaugh, regarded as the last surviving portions of ancient oak wood, were declared a Site of Special Scientific Interest, and in 1969 part of this area was leased by Nottinghamshire County Council as a country park. The Sherwood Forest Visitor Centre was opened in 1976, and a walk to see the Major Oak became a must for visitors, young and old alike. The international importance of the ancient oaks, wood pasture and heathland was recognised in 2002 with the establishment of the Sherwood Forest National Nature Reserve which covers over 420 hectares of Birklands and Budby Forests. There are currently exciting plans to develop new visitor facilities including a discovery centre and tree top walkways to view the forest.

Another part of the old forest has been planted with conifers and this forms the Sherwood Pines Forest Park. This has a completely different character with its blocks of tall straight trees, but the forest rides are well used by walkers and cyclists, while the 'Go Ape' high wire adventure course of rope bridges, swings and zip slides is aimed at those seeking a more exhilarating experience.

Edwinstowe is situated at the heart of Robin Hood country and it was here that the legendary hero supposedly married Maid Marian. Nearby Ollerton grew up where several major routes crossed the River Maun but, like many of the settlements in the area, it underwent rapid expansion in the 1920s as a colliery village. Worksop and Retford are both thriving historic market towns, and there are some very attractive estate villages in and around the Dukeries. Bestwood was once a royal hunting park within Sherwood Forest but it is now a Country Park, while the house and gardens at Newstead Abbey, once the home of the poet Lord Byron, are also open to visitors. The Great North Road, with its historic coaching inns, passed through the forest, while the Chesterfield Canal, linking Derbyshire to the River Trent, winds its way through the northern part of the region.

We have spent a year visiting the towns and villages of 'Robin Hood Country', and the many woods and parks that give the area its unique character. We hope you will be inspired by our photographs to come and enjoy the many attractive and interesting places on offer. And when you get here why not leave your car behind and use the extensive network of cycle trails, bridleways and footpaths to explore and get close to nature.

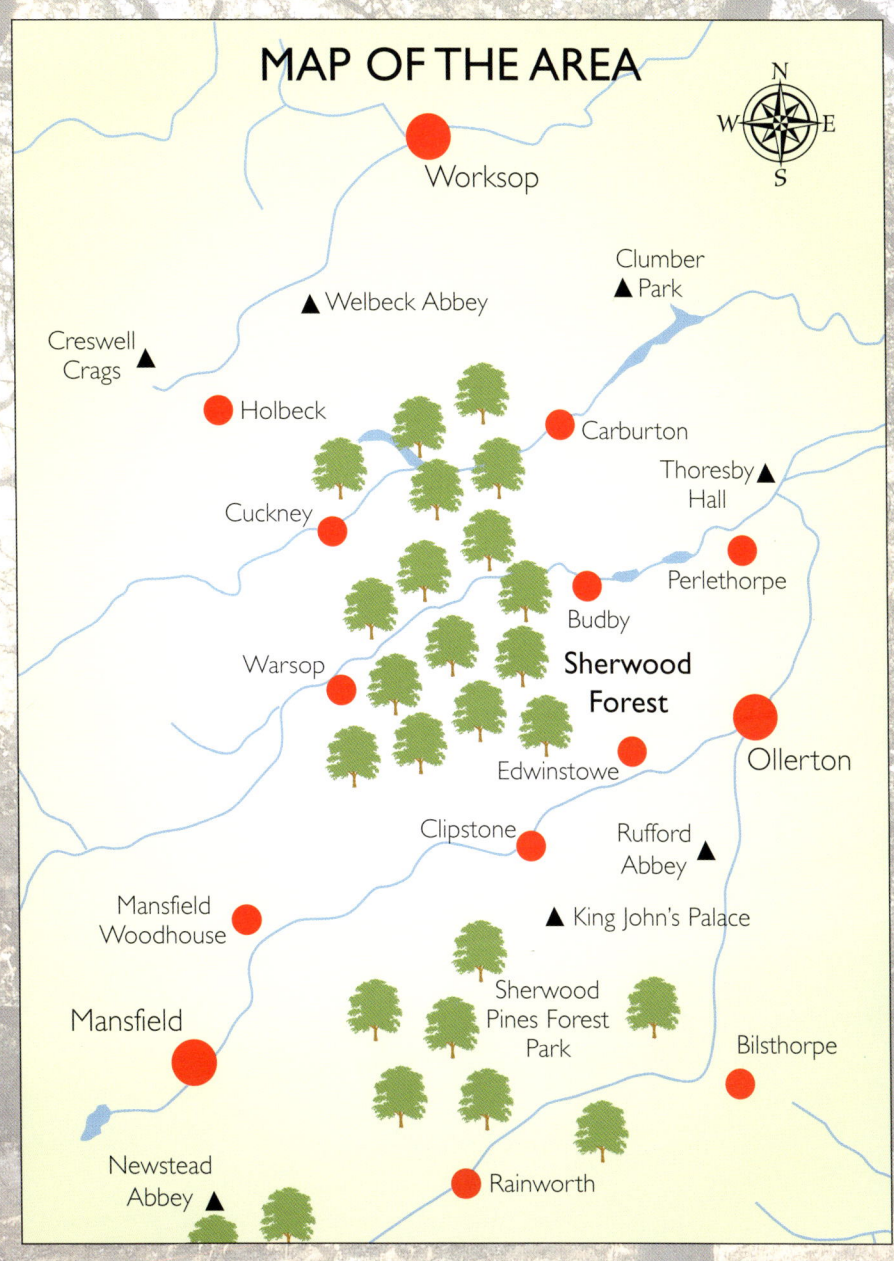

MAP OF THE AREA

Worksop

Clumber
▲ Park

▲ Welbeck Abbey

Creswell
Crags ▲

Holbeck

Carburton

Thoresby ▲
Hall

Cuckney

Perlethorpe

Budby

Warsop

**Sherwood
Forest**

Ollerton

Edwinstowe

Clipstone

Rufford
Abbey ▲

Mansfield
Woodhouse

▲ King John's Palace

Mansfield

Sherwood
Pines Forest
Park

Bilsthorpe

Newstead
Abbey ▲

Rainworth

Visitors to Sherwood Forest
Every young visitor to Sherwood Forest becomes a member of Robin Hood's band of outlaws.

Sherwood Forest Visitor Centre
The legendary figures of Robin Hood and Little John form the centrepiece at the busy Visitor Centre.

**In the Footsteps
of Robin Hood**
Display panels, shaped
like a longbow, can be found
at twelve locations in Robin Hood
country. This display is at
Creswell Crags.

Opposite page:
With maps, illustrations and
stories, the interpretation panels
give visitors more information
on the Robin Hood legends.
These pictures are from the
displays at Edwinstowe
church, Sherwood Forest and
Thieves Wood.

Daffodils
A display of daffodils, as seen here in the gardens at Rufford Country Park,
cheer everyone and show that winter is losing its grip and spring has arrived.

Opposite page: **Beech buds**
In spring the trees of the forest seem to come alive as buds burst open and new leaves emerge.

Oak seedling
A young oak starts its long journey within the decaying trunk of one of its ancestors in Sherwood Forest.

Dead oak
Evening sunshine highlights the dead trunk of this ancient oak tree, which now provides a valuable home to many insect species.

The clock tower of Thoresby Hall
In winter sunshine the clock tower of Thoresby Hall shows clearly through the open wrought-iron gates.

Cherry blossom at Thoresby
In spring cherry blossom forms
a floral avenue leading up to the Hall.

Bluebells
A carpet of bluebells, seen here under beech trees in Clumber Park, is surely one of the spectacles of spring.

Truman's Lodge
This attractive arched building stands at one of the entrances into Clumber Park.

Clumber Bridge
The semi-circular arches of the bridge are reflected in the still waters of Clumber Lake.
The bridge was built in 1763 for the Duke of Newcastle.

Potato planting
The light soils of this region have proved to be excellent for vegetable growing,
and in spring many fields are planted with potatoes.

Bed forming
Here flat 'beds' of fine soil are carefully prepared and stones are removed,
ready for the sowing of vegetable crops like carrots and onions.

Hardwick Village
The village of Hardwick, built within
Clumber Park in the nineteenth and
early twentieth centuries to house estate
staff, is seen beyond a brilliant yellow
field of flowering oil-seed rape.

The Lime Avenue in spring
The double avenue of lime trees is one of the main attractions for visitors driving through Clumber Park.
The original trees date from the early nineteenth century but the avenue has been extended with
further plantings during the last half of the twentieth century.

Lime leaves
These are the heart-shaped leaves of the European lime, which is a hybrid that was planted
extensively in the past in private and municipal parks and gardens.

Bracken fronds
Bracken is a plant that is found on acidic soils in woods and heaths, and in spring it grows very fast,
its branching green fronds soon reaching the height of a man.

Opposite: **Rhododendron flowers**
In the past rhododendron was widely planted in the gardens of large country houses. Although its
vigorous and invasive growth has made it something of a pest, its exotic flowers are very pretty.

Sherwood Forest in early summer
Sherwood Forest is dominated by oak trees, along with other native species like birch, rowan, holly and hawthorn.

Sherwood Forest National Nature Reserve
The last remaining fragment of the great forest of Sherwood is now being managed as a National Nature Reserve.

Cyclists in Sherwood Forest
Cyclists can enjoy traffic-free paths and quiet lanes throughout the Sherwood area. National Route 6, linking Derby and York, is part of the National Cycle Network and it passes through the heart of Robin Hood country.

Sherwood Pines Forest Park
The Forest Park has many facilities for cyclists, including a busy cycle-hire centre and trails to suit everyone from the adventurous mountain-biker to the leisurely family group.

Raindrops
A brief shower is sufficient to empty the refreshment tables at Rufford Country Park,
but the re-appearance of the sun makes everywhere sparkle.

Raindrops
Raindrops are caught in the attractive leaves of lady's mantle in the gardens at Rufford Country Park.

Stormy skies
The combination of sunshine and dark skies lends atmosphere to this view of Thoresby Hall,
once a stately home but now an historic hotel.

Dark clouds
Dark clouds are reflected in the lake in this panoramic view of Newstead Abbey.

This page:
Caves at Creswell Crags

Opposite page:
Creswell Crags
Creswell Crags is a limestone gorge honeycombed with caves that were used by prehistoric man many thousands of years ago. Robin Hood's Cave is the largest of the caves and it may have provided shelter for Robin Hood and his outlaws. All the caves have metal grilles to protect their archaeology but they can be explored as part of a guided cave tour.

Blyth
Archway House is in the centre of a row of old cottages on the side of Blyth's picturesque village green.

Blyth
The ancient church tower can be seen beyond the crossroads, with the white-painted
Fourways Hotel situated opposite the blue-painted Craft Studio.

Carrot beds
The long parallel beds of carrots stretch up to the skyline with its lone tree in this field near Rainsworth.

King John's Palace, Clipstone
The surviving ruins are a very small part of a royal palace once used by the Plantagenet kings.
King John and Richard the Lionheart stayed here when they were hunting in the forest.

View of Edwinstowe
Edwinstowe, named after Edwin,
ruler of the ancient kingdom of
Northumbria, is situated at the heart
of Robin Hood country. Once a small
village, it expanded rapidly in the
1920s when Thoresby Colliery
was opened.

Forest Corner, Edwinstowe
Throughout the summer months Edwinstowe Cricket Club plays
matches on one of the most attractive grounds in the county.

Funfair at Forest Corner
Also open throughout the summer, the funfair gives children the chance
to enjoy the many rides and test their skills at the various stalls.

Reflections
A feeding moorhen and the leaves of reedmace are reflected in the cool waters of the River Poulter.

The steeple of Clumber Chapel
The tall steeple of the chapel
at Clumber is reflected in the lake
in this evening view taken
from the bridge.

Summer pines

The tall straight trunks of the pine trees show that this is a plantation, one of many established in the Sherwood area, but here the canopy is sufficiently open to allow an under storey of bracken, rosebay willow-herb and fine grasses to grow.

Summer oak
A veteran oak basks in the sun in Sherwood Forest.

Clumber Chapel
Although the great mansion at Clumber was demolished in 1938 the chapel remains.
It was built in the 1880s in the Gothic style for the Duke of Newcastle and has been
described as a miniature cathedral.

Right:
The stableyard at Clumber
Once every large country house had its stableyard providing accommodation
for the horses, carriages and grooms. Although no longer required for this purpose,
the buildings now house the National Trust gift shops and restaurant.

Oak leaves
The beautiful patterns of cells and veins are revealed in this close-up photograph of oak leaves.

Oak leaves and acorns
Acorns, the seeds of the oak tree, grow throughout the summer, before falling to the ground in autumn.

Robin Hood signs
When the name Robin Hood was adopted for the new Doncaster Sheffield airport it was quite
controversial as the airport is in the county of South Yorkshire, not Nottinghamshire.
But the publicity has been beneficial and the name is easy to remember.

Opposite page:
Many local businesses, like these in Edwinstowe, use the Robin Hood connection to promote themselves.

QUALITY GIFTS

☎ (01623) 824117

ROBIN'S DEN

ROBIN HOOD
PLAICE
QUALITY
FISH & CHIPS
KEBABS
PIZZAS
Eat-in or Take-Away

Maid
Marian
Restaurant
& Bar
01623 822266
CAR PARK ➜

Summer view near Osberton
Summer skies enhance this
view over Rayton Farm with
golden fields of stubble and
green fields of sugar beet.

Summer view in Clumber Park
Two tall silver birch trees edge this view across an area of open grass and heath in Clumber Park, with the unmistakeable silhouette of Clumber Chapel on the horizon.

Oats and a tree
A field of golden oats stands
ready for harvesting under a
sky of wispy clouds.

Heather in flower
When in flower, heather is not only attractive to
look at, but it provides a valuable nectar source
for bees and other insects.

Heathland at Budby
In late summer the purple-flowering heather
turns the heathland at Budby a glorious colour.

Sherwood Pines Forest Park
The café is just one of the many facilities on offer to visitors at Sherwood Pines, the largest forest park in the Midlands.

Sherwood Forest Art and Craft Centre
Built in 1859 as the coach house and stables to Edwinstowe Hall, and later used as a dormitory by
Bolsover Colliery, the buildings have now been converted into an art and craft centre. The central glazed
atrium ensures that visitors can wander between the various studios and the café whatever the weather.

Summer grasses
Evening sunshine highlights the golden heads of flowering grasses.

Longhorn cattle
A herd of English longhorn cattle, a traditional breed, have been introduced to parts of Sherwood Forest
to graze the under storey and help recreate the wood pasture that was once an important habitat.

Baling straw
Dust flies on a hot summer day as a tractor and baler collect up the straw after harvesting.

Harvesting corn
A trailer is filled with corn from the combine harvester at the end of another busy day.

The Courtyard at Thoresby Hall
Four large planters grouped around a statue of Robin Hood form the centrepiece in the old stable-yard at Thoresby Hall, which has been converted into a gallery, tea room and craft shops.

Newstead Abbey
Famous as the home of the romantic poet Lord Byron, the house was created from the earlier
monastic buildings, and it includes the ruined west front of the abbey church.

Moving water
Sunlight catches a sheet of water as it flows over the outfall
from the lake at Newstead Abbey.

The River Poulter flows over a bed of bricks to form the ford in Clumber Park.
While walkers can cross a foot-bridge, cars must drive through the shallow water.

Greenhouses in the walled garden
Productive walled gardens were a
feature of large country houses in
the nineteenth and early twentieth
centuries, and greenhouses were built
along the south-facing walls so that
exotic crops of fruit, vegetables and
flowers could be grown.

Iron floor grille
Ferns grow in the relative cool and shade under the ornate iron grilles that form the path through the greenhouses.

**The Sculpture Collection
at Rufford**
A number of large pieces of
contemporary outdoor sculpture
are displayed in The Orangery
and within the formal gardens
at Rufford Country Park.

**'Man and Ewe
on a Park Bench'**
This amusing sculpture by
Sioban Coppinger must bring a
smile to the face of everyone
who sees and sits on it.

Rowan berries
A view of the woodland floor as the first berries and leaves of autumn begin to fall.

A miniature landscape
A close-up view of the strange shapes of lichens and mosses, growing on an old tree stump in the forest.

The A1
Road numbering and classification began in the 1920s when the A1 became the main route between London and Edinburgh. It is the modern replacement for the Great North Road and takes traffic through Robin Hood country.

The East Coast railway line
The main railway line linking London to Edinburgh follows a similar route to the A1
as it passes through the area, with some trains stopping at Retford station.

The Chesterfield Canal
The canal runs for about forty-six miles from Chesterfield in Derbyshire to Stockwith on the River Trent, passing through Worksop and Retford. Here a narrowboat is moored at Forest Middle Top Lock.

Forest Top Lock on the Chesterfield Canal
Completed in 1777 and intended for the carriage of heavy goods like stone, coal and bricks, the canal fell out of use in the mid twentieth century. It is now being restored and facilities provided for boating, angling, cycling and walking.

Sulphur tuft fungus
Named for its sulphur-yellow colour, this fungus is commonly found on decaying and rotten wood.

Autumn tints
Bright sunshine highlights the first autumn tints in the bracken.

Norton
This quiet little village nestles to the south of Welbeck Park.

The Greendale Oak

The public house in Cuckney takes its name from a famous tree in Welbeck Park. It was the largest oak in the area and was capable of having a coach and horses driven through it, although sadly it has now gone.

Welbeck monument

A lone cyclist takes a well-earned break at the Welbeck monument. It was constructed to celebrate the memory of Lord George Bentinck, a Member of Parliament and the third son of the 4th Duke of Portland, who died near this spot in 1848.

Welbeck Estate cottage
This is one of many ornamental lodges that are found on the access roads into Welbeck Estate.

Cuckney church tower
Two doves look out from the belfry above the clock on the church tower.

Cuckney church
The ancient church of St Mary
is viewed from the churchyard.

Silver birch trees in autumn
A clump of mature silver birches stand in autumn sunshine in Sherwood Forest.

Birch logs
A pile of silver birch logs has been left to decay.

Waterfowl on Rufford Lake
Mute swans, Canada and Greylag geese gather for an early morning feed on Rufford Lake.

Vapour trails
Vapour trails from passing aircraft are mirrored in the still waters of the Great Lake in Welbeck Park.

Winding gear at Clipstone mine
Although it was once an important area for the deep mining of coal, the abandoned winding gear at Clipstone symbolises the contraction of the industry that has been such a feature of the late twentieth century.

Thoresby Colliery entrance
Part of a winding wheel has been used at the entrance to Thoresby Colliery, on the outskirts of Edwinstowe,
one of the few working coal mines remaining in Nottinghamshire.

Rufford Abbey
Early morning sunshine casts long shadows across the grounds of Rufford Abbey.

Toadstools
These enormous toadstools are a sculpture by Peter Randall-Page,
part of the collection displayed in the gardens at Rufford Country Park.

The Hop Pole Hotel
The Hop Pole Hotel in Ollerton is an old coaching inn and its name is a reminder
of the hop-growing industry which once flourished in the area.

Ollerton Watermill
The watermill still contains a working mill-wheel but it also hosts an award-winning tea shop.

Tuxford Windmill
The four-storey tower mill has been fully restored and its working machinery can be viewed by visitors.
There is also a mill shop selling flour ground at the mill, and a tea shop.

Oil well near Bothamsall

The first commercial oil field in the country was at Eakring and it began producing oil in 1939. Although this site has now been closed, 'nodding donkeys' can still be seen in the area, pumping oil up from underground.

Sherwood Forest in autumn
Leaves cover the bridleway that passes through Sherwood Forest, linking Edwinstowe and Budby.

The Robin Hood Way
This long distance path runs from Nottingham Castle to Edwinstowe church, linking all
the places in Nottinghamshire that are associated with the Robin Hood legends.

Village sign
The sign for Bothamsall depicts the church and castle mound, alongside a wheatsheaf and cricket stump representing the farming community at work and play.

Castle mound
The tree-studded mound of a Norman castle is located at the entrance to the village of Bothamsall.

Boughton Pumping Station
In the Victorian and Edwardian era several pumping stations were built in this area to extract
water from the underlying sandstone beds. Now obsolete, the tall engine-house chimney at
Boughton Pumping Station rises above the surrounding trees.

The Lime Avenue in autumn
Autumn sunshine highlights the glorious colours of the leaves on the lime trees in part of the avenue in Clumber Park.

Edwinstowe
The medieval church of St Mary is reputed to be the setting for the wedding of Robin Hood and Maid Marian. The tall spire is a prominent feature in the area.

Edwinstowe
The meeting of Robin Hood and Maid Marian
is depicted on the sign for Edwinstowe, and by a statue
placed outside the public library on the High Street.

Longhorn cattle at Thoresby
As the weather deteriorates and grass stops growing so extra feed is
put out for the longhorn cattle in the park at Thoresby.

Harvesting onions
A tractor and trailer collects a load of onions in this harvesting scene near Budby.

Frosted leaves
A single yellow birch leaf has fallen onto frosted oak leaves.

Tree stump
The upturned stump of an old oak tree makes a natural sculpture in Sherwood Forest.

Papplewick Pumping Station
The main building at this Victorian pumping station houses two massive beam engines that pumped water up from a deep well to fill a reservoir that served the city of Nottingham. Visitors are welcome on Sunday afternoons to view the ornate architecture, and the pumps are 'in steam' on bank holidays.

Thieves Wood, near Blidworth
The old route north from Nottingham, known as the King's Way, passed through Thieves Wood.
It is thought that the fate of unfortunate travellers upon the road gave the wood its name.

Winter sun
Rays of winter sun stream through this old oak tree in Sherwood Forest.

Pine trees in winter
The slanting rays of the winter sun light up the frosted bramble leaves
under the conifers in this plantation near Clumber.

The Harley Gallery
This award winning gallery features a range of contemporary arts and crafts together with a museum,
shop and coffee bar, all built on the site of the former gasworks of Welbeck Estate.

The Dukeries Garden Centre
The garden centre has been established within the extensive Victorian walled garden of
the Welbeck Estate, and it incorporates many of the original glass houses.

Carburton church
The church is small and plain but the tiny original windows and round arches suggest that it dates from the Norman period. It is unusual in that the exterior stonework is covered by a layer of cement plaster.

Round stable at Thoresby
This unique stable building dates from the late nineteenth century.
It has ten stables around a small central yard but it is now used for plant sales.

Robin Hood sign
The Robin Hood is a popular public house and restaurant on the crossroads at Lidgett, near Edwinstowe.

Ye Olde Bell Hotel at Barnby Moor
This is one of the coaching inns on the old Great North Road where travellers warmed
themselves at huge log fires while drinking glasses of steaming punch.

123

Go Ape
This course of rope bridges, tarzan swings and zip slides high up in the trees of
Sherwood Pines Forest Park is for those seeking fun and adventure.

Logging
A pile of sawn timber is stacked at the roadside in Sherwood Pines Forest Park.

Giant Rabbits
Two giant rabbit sculptures wait under a tree at Rufford Country Park.

Ruins at Rufford Abbey
Bare branches and the dark outline of the ruins at Rufford Abbey create a forbidding image.

Retford Market Square
Bright sunshine lights up the Market Square and the red and blue canopies of the empty stalls.

Market stall
Shoppers are busy stocking up on fresh vegetables at this stall in Retford Market.

The Major Oak

The Major Oak, named after Major Rooke who first described it in a book published in 1790, could be as much as 800 years old. Its massive trunk is 10 m (33 feet) in circumference making it the largest tree still standing in the Sherwood area. It has long attracted visitors and its hollow trunk is reputed to have been the hiding place for Robin Hood and his Merry Men. Because of its unique importance the tree has been protected by a number of conservation measures. Visitors are prevented from trampling the ground around the trunk and it has a support system of poles and wires to ensure its continued existence.

Perlethorpe
These attractive houses are part of Perlethorpe, a small village within Thoresby Estate. The houses were
built in the mid nineteenth century for workers on the estate's farms, forests and woodyard.

Gate post
Look closely and you will see that the decorative tops to the gate posts on the Thoresby Estate are not stone, but wood.

Church Warsop
The church of St Peter and St Paul gives Church Warsop its name. It lies on the
north bank of the River Meden while Market Warsop lies on the south bank.

The Mill Dam at Church Warsop
Waterfowl collect near the Mill Dam on the River Meden. The nearby
water meadows, known as The Carrs, are a local nature reserve.

135

The Priory Gatehouse

Worksop Priory
The Priory church dates from the twelfth century when it was part of the Augustinian monastery. After the Dissolution of the Monasteries it became the parish church for the town. The Priory Gatehouse is an important survival from the fourteenth century. Originally it guarded the entrance into the medieval monastery.

The Priory Shopping Centre at Worksop
The modern Priory Shopping Centre off Bridge Street is the focus for retail activity in the
town centre, its name reflecting the town's historic past.

Frosted grass
Frost has transformed the heathland, but it is already disappearing under the winter sun.

Melting frost
Sunlight is melting the frost and lighting up the droplets of water.

Floodlit trees
At Christmas coloured floodlights transform the trees in the gardens at Rufford Country Park and create a magical setting.

Sunset at Apleyhead Gate
The outline of the greyhounds which form part of the arms of the Dukes of Newcastle can be
seen over the central archway of Apleyhead Gate, one of the entrances into Clumber Park.

Sunset over Thoresby Hall
The setting sun lights up a vapour trail, and a wisp of cloud looks like smoke from the chimneys of Thoresby Hall.

Ancient oaks
For hundreds of years these veteran oak trees have been growing in Sherwood Forest;
their huge knobbly trunks stand as evidence of their great age.